Spirituality is not a sanctuary from ordeal, but the realm in which all that could be envisioned and internally experienced within human possibility can be realized.

Human Natures

Human Natures

OF ANIMAL
AND SPIRITUAL

Carroll Blair

Aveon Publishing Company

Printed in the United States of America

ISBN: 978-1-936430-07-9

Library of Congress Control Number: 2010912395

Aveon Publishing Co.
P.O. Box 381570
Cambridge, MA   02238-1570 USA

Also by author

Grains of Thought
Facing the Circle
Reel to Real
Shifting Tides
Reaches
Quarter Notes
Poetics
Out of Silence
By Rays of Light
Into the Inner Life
Gnosis of the Heart
Soul Reflections
Beneath and Beyond the Surface
Of Courage and Commitment
For Today and Tomorrow
In Meditation
Sightings Along the Journey
Through Desert's Fire
Offerings to Pilgrims
Atoms from the Suns of Solitude
Colors of Devotion

To all who go the journey to light
in a world still deep in the dark

Prologue

From the beginnings of the human species
the animal of its constitution was fully
present in impulse and operation, and being
of a harsh environment of the wild, was
necessary to its survival. Manifestation of a
spiritual power appeared some time later,
though still before recorded history — expressions of art such as early cave paintings
and what they portrayed in vision and
human depth showing that there was more
to humankind than just animal inclination.
The meandering road toward civilization,
however much the ideal rather than an ac-
complished reality, further demonstrated
human need for something nobler than what
animal existence had to provide, some from
cultures of antiquity exploring greater dimen-
sions of human-being, intimating profound
distinctions that distinguished humanity from
the rest of the animal world — if it was willing
to forgo the ego-ridden goals of the temporal
and turn its attention to the direction of the
spiritual, realizing the human world is still
very much an animal world, and that human
evolution and spiritual evolution are one.

Human Natures
of Animal and Spiritual

It cannot be said that man is a spiritual being
until he begins to live through the higher
nature that is available to human life — he
is a living, spiritual entity only in potential —
if he wills to be . . . works to be.

What brings physical life into being is of the
animal, which is right and natural, but it is
the animal of human character that thwarts
the rising of human spiritual life.

Individuals have been shown to grow in
wisdom throughout the course of their lives,
but a critique of human history reveals that
this has not been so for humankind as a
whole, one generation after another making
the same mistakes, cumbered by the same

follies that dominate human existence, played out through its animal nature from one age to the next, the only true change or difference being the means by which to express them, failing to achieve a sustainable advance in spiritual progression.

As eroding as CO_2 gasses are to the ozone layer is animality to the health of human life when venturing outside the physical.

Animals throughout Nature are driven by the will to survive, satisfying hungers and appetites belonging to their species, the spur to get them gratified and methods of procurement selfish in character, but here, excusable, because it is what they must do and are incapable of doing anything else, essential to their survival and decreed by the governing force that moves their lives,

unlike the selfishness so often present in
human-being, which cannot be excused, for
it is able to ascend to something higher by
grace of its spiritual nature.

It can clearly be seen in the operations of
human affairs how great the difference as
well as distance is between the actions in
accord with high ideals and principles
and those of the lower nature (the latter
more often triumphant in trumping
the nobler way).

It is what man does beyond what he needs
to do to meet the needs of survival where
his contribution to life or crimes against
life begin.

Human Natures

Noble character cannot be without living through and guided by the spiritual of one's being.

An error that is often made is for one to move his life outward before moving inward, making his way to his spiritual nature, to his source of power and light.

There is cunning, scheming, gaming, but no excellence in human animality beyond expressions of the body.

Animal nature is harmonious in human life only when it doesn't transgress its place, and doesn't move to dominate.

of Animal and Spiritual

Every time the baser course is chosen over
the higher, the world is betrayed.

Humankind is not meant to dwell in the lower
stratums of its constitution but ascend to the
highest, for a species succeeds to the extent
that it lives up to its highest strength.

The law of the jungle, or the way of the
light . . . this is the choice that must be made.

Dark is any day in a human life when used
for the pursuit of the base.

Human Natures

The most menacing ailment of the human species is not cancer, or acquired immune deficiency syndrome, or heart disease, or a multitude of other conditions that endanger its life, but ego, doing the bidding of the lower nature.

The dominance of animality over man is the proverbial elephant in the room that must be seriously addressed if man is to move forward in a true and substantive way.

Of the disputes that are decided in the human world a majority are resolved through less than noble means — if not by bellicosity, then guile, dissimulation, and other features of animal nature, whatever parties involved trying to get the better of the other(s), thinking only of their own interests, not concerned with what is fair and just for all in question.

Where the spiritual is in operation rules are unnecessary as to how to be just and do right by others.

In education one does not enter college before going to elementary school, yet many go into the world in pursuit of careers with college degrees without even an elementary development of the spiritual dimension of their lives.

How effective are they in their service to other than themselves . . . this, the concern of the noble of spirit.

Principles of the higher order can have little meaning or definition beyond abstraction for one living under rule of the lower nature.

Human Natures

Love, compassion, kindness; a sense of
justice independent of all law and dogma;
an instinctive knowledge of what is right
and good . . . these attributes are of the life
lived through the higher nature.

As long as one is motivated by selfishness
he is of little value to others and even less
to himself, for it obstructs all means of
inner movement from animal to spiritual,
where establishing a life of truth and higher
purpose must begin.

The spiritual is more concerned with
saving and protecting than being saved
and protected.

of Animal and Spiritual

The instinct for self-preservation is stronger in animal nature than it is in the spiritual, because the spiritual is selfless, and animality is all about self.

In human animal it is utility that binds one to another; in the spiritual it is love.

What does it mean to live through the higher nature in regard to others? To never do anything to another that would be ignoble or knowingly improper, nothing that would encroach upon another's rights or violate his or her life in any way, no matter how much gain there would be for oneself, or how immune from retribution.

Human Natures

The subtle doings of human animal nature in the world are more pervasive and destructive than the outbursts of violence or aggression.

The lower nature knows nothing of selfless service, its focus being on manipulation to its service.

All is contrived in the life that has not realized the spiritual.

Without wisdom and courage love cannot be, and much of what passes for love is (as saccharine to sugar) a substitute for the real thing.

of Animal and Spiritual

Even among the forms of human relations
considered to be the closest, motives of a   .
misleading character could be revealed.

What falls short of noble conduct falls to the
animal side of human-being.

The right direction to go or the right thing
to do is what is opposite to the proddings
of ego.

Consideration for others in all aspects of
association is a rarer virtue than most
would care to believe.

Human Natures

Every discerning person asks himself or
herself before entering into a relationship:
"Is this person good for me?" But the noble
of spirit ask an additional question and make
the decision according to the answer, which
is: "Am I good for this person; could I be a
positive in his or her life, never to impede
the potential companion in aspiring to his
or her best?"

The difference between the mind-set of
the one whose focus is on using people and
one whose attention is on helping people is
(literally) the difference between night
and day.

Only the spiritual provides the sensitivity
and imagination to share in the experiences

of others in ways removed from the shallow, transcending the limitations of the senses attending the physical. Only those who are able to feel and reflect deeply can appreciate the joy, the love, the pains and sorrows of another with a comprehension that is beyond reach of the lower nature.

When one living through the higher nature is with others, one makes one's life (one's time) about others; when alone, the concentration is on mining the treasure within (to give to others).

For the animal, everything is outside, to be used and exploited for mean interests. For the spiritual, its universe is within, where treasure is ever lighting, ready to serve.

Human Natures

Some people achieve a little, then believe
they've earned the right to abuse others.
Some achieve much, and hope they are
then worthy to be of service.

Gifts of the temporal such as physical beauty,
privileged heritage or class advantage are
more a test than they are a gift — what will
one do with them (or not do with them) . . .
will they foster kindness and gratitude, or
arrogance and conceit; empathy and compassion, or a self-centeredness that leads
to an abusive temperament? Moving one
closer to or further from what is of true
importance — what gives human life its
value and distinction beyond all animals.

of Animal and Spiritual

Worldly ambitions fiercely pursued concretize base traits of character and weaken or eliminate the virtuous.

Animal nature can "rise" to the top of the worldly, but here it is truly an Alice in Wonderland scenario: what seems up, is down; what seems good, is bad; what seems right, is wrong.

The spiritual sells nothing of itself, nor is it interested in buying or selling anything of the souls of others.

Human Natures

Ego is the great trickster, for it leads its subject into believing that his life is expanding, when it is really narrowing.

If one driven by the lower nature were to suddenly have everything that he wanted, he would soon feel as though he had nothing. (Would know, then, that what he was longing for was empty.)

Ego is creative in nothing but delusions, carrying images of self-worth and importance that ever fall short of the truth.

No structure of ego-oriented society is absent of baseness and falsity, and nothing

honorable can be built upon a foundation
that is base or false.

Principled intent manifests from a generous
and humble heart, beyond the realm of
animal-natured life.

One is more than what one does only when
living through the spiritual of one's being.

One can go far in worldly pursuits without
knowledge or skill beyond average save to
exploit the innocence and credulity of others,
ever prepared with trick or machination
to get the better of the unsuspecting.

Human Natures

Where one learns cunning, shrewdness,
deception, strategy to further ego-interest
is not a place whose character is noble
(or where expressions of noble character
are encouraged).

Throughout the world of careerism animal
nature is well endorsed, not in name or
description, but the characteristics of raw
ambition for power and position, the
expedient approach to plan and action to
achieve ego-driven goals encouraged without misgivings, and though often subtle,
the message is clear — that in this world
[this arena] such conduct is rewarded.

Corruption is at the core of the worldly, and
animal nature at the core of corruption.

of Animal and Spiritual

Interests compelled by the lower nature
go after the loaf and let the crumbs fall
where they may.

Like the nature from which it comes, the
interest of greed is narrow, its vision, short —
profit at any cost — the consequences, long.

The animal of human-being is without
humility, and nothing is more lost than a
human life without humility.

With closed eyes the spiritual can go in
light; with open eyes the animal outside
the corporal can only go in darkness.

Human Natures

The essentials of life would be in ample
supply for all if not for the disease of avarice
known only to the human species, the
wanting in ceaseless want of non-essentials,
compromising the quality of present and
future life for all.

Mortal death makes any selfish or greedy act
all the more absurd, for, being of the fleeting,
it invariably comes to nothing, the temporal
life able to escape futility only by fusion
with the spiritual.

The ego-ridden mind tends to the temporal
as if it were forever and pays no attention
to what is right and true.

of Animal and Spiritual

Greed taken to its end is like a man on his
death bed clutching wads of paper money,
weeping in anguish because he must part
with them as others around him look on
with sorrow.

Who feeds the animal of his being becomes
less as it devours more.

When living through animality much goes
to waste, limiting possibility; when living
through the spiritual nothing is wasted,
fielding a world of open possibility.

Animal nature shackles; the spiritual
liberates.

Human Natures

To choose the animal over the spiritual is like having a chance to fly but choosing to crawl.

In the spiritual, surrender does not mean to be vanquished, but to enter into a new state of consciousness unattainable to the heretofore life of ego.

Spirituality is not so much a giving up of the worldly as it is a letting go of the unreal.

Who lives through the higher nature is not concerned with managing a pretense of image, but a progression of inner growth.

of Animal and Spiritual

It is infinitely more important to transcend
the animal of one's being than to escape
from some region of the earth to have the
opportunity to live a rich and powerful life.

What is of truth cannot be seen nor heard
nor felt by the life held in the grip of the
lower nature.

Animality does not *live*, it merely exists
(as all that cannot transcend the temporal
can only exist).

The purposeful life is by one means or other
a contribution of light — realized in union
with the spiritual.

Only by turning away from ego and its legion of strivings does one reveal oneself to be serious about the spiritual path.

The breakthrough in human development is going from finite mind to infinite mind; from animal human to spiritual human.

It is a presumption to consider oneself born into life as a spiritual being without having made the journey or engaging the work necessary to actualize a living spirituality.

There are those regarding the spiritual journey like the runner who jumps in near the end of the race, running ahead to declare victory, fraudulent in his rush for glory as the true participants are doing their best to go the distance, the impostor pretending to be among them, wanting to hear cheers from the crowd, to receive an acclamation that he hasn't a right to, not knowing the primary lesson for all who journey the spiritual path — that it is not about pride or vainglory fueled by the lower nature, but the challenge, the test, the steeling of one's resolve to expel from one's life what is bound in ego to make way for the principal goal of spiritual endeavor — the fulfillment of selfless giving.

The glorious is ever beautiful, but never the eye [what is behind the eye] that lusts for glory.

The world is warmed by spiritual passions; burned by passions of animality that rove outside the corporal.

However aggressive or assertive animal nature may sometimes be, it is never free of fear — of losing what it has or not getting what it wants.

The spiritual uses materiality as it is needed, without obsession. Obsession with materialism is the province of animal nature.

The lower nature is rife with ungratified desires, and without qualms about interfering with the needs of one or another in its quest to satisfy them.

Avarice, covetousness, are among the worst of company to a human life, needing to be banished before substantive inner growth can commence.

Freedom cannot be where there is pre-occupation with appetites that cannot be fulfilled — it can only be known (and lived) through the spiritual dimension.

Before the mind is free, before the heart is free, the door to humility must open.

Human Natures

The irony of the self-centered life is that
what it wants, or doesn't want to part with
is of the fleeting, and thus, of fantasy (as
all is fantasy that is not of the everlasting).

What doesn't operate through the spiritual
is sanctioned by folly.

The quarry of the lower nature may be
for a time, stimulating, but not uplifting
or inspiring.

The worldly offers only what enslaves.

of Animal and Spiritual

Animal nature is about attachment; the
spiritual, detachment — but with great
compassion and love.

The state of selflessness is a state of grace.

One cannot contribute in a significant way
until (unless) one is detached from animal
impulse beyond the physical, for then it is
not about ego, motivated by fears or private
interests, but of other, all action and gesture
performed in the spirit of selflessness, the
heart of the spiritual.

A life lived through the spiritual uses its
strength to open, to acquire, to create
only for the purpose of giving.

Human Natures

Where the heart is good the life from which it serves can only be the same.

Salvation in the spiritual has a meaning counter to that of saving oneself in the temporal. In the spiritual, one is willing to be transformed so something within can evolve to a nobility in offering of service to what is other than (and greater than) oneself. "Saving oneself" in the temporal means doing everything one can to hold on to illusions of what one believes himself to be, ready to abandon integrity and betray any virtue if it is what it will take to continue his ego-driven existence without change.

Positive change in human life transpires through the dismantling of ego, but if it is to morph into greater change (i.e. greater growth) a sincere questioning and evaluation

of where one is in the commitment to
spiritual development must ever be
in play.

An infant has the purity and innocence
of spirituality, but that is all, save for the
potential to grow from animal human to
spiritual human. To realize its promise
it must be studious throughout its life
in the work of higher growth.

Beyond the seeking of fleeting pleasures
and glory is creating a worthiness of the
gift of life.

Of grand structure are the pyramids, built
a stone at a time . . . and so it is with the

building of spiritual character — one step
at a time, one trial at a time.

The capital of the true kingdom is not made
of earthly riches, but spiritual courage.

Some have humble moments which draw
them inward, beginning the work necessary
for transformation, but it is not sustained;
after a brief time they fall back into errant
ways and allow the lower nature to again
take charge of their lives.

They are in a sense already dead who turn
their lives over to the lower nature, roaming
the land of the dying.

of Animal and Spiritual

The spiritual life is lived with a recognition that it is never about one's self, and not for sale at any price.

The deeds of a human being are the ornaments of his or her ideals.

The face of the worldly is not of the spiritual.

Ego demands a crown as it goes about in chains.

Human Natures

The spiritual seeks no honors, no favors, no
special rights — only to do what is right.

Only the lower nature can be impressed with
anything of a worldly character.

There are paths in life that no matter what
is achieved the whole amounts to nothing,
because integrity did not show anywhere
or in any thing.

In the marketplace of promotional enterprise
are frequent productions of fraud, of pretense,
of artifice, of mediocrity; self-indulgent, self-
exalting, self-serving, false in exhibition or
claim, the lower nature central to the activity.

of Animal and Spiritual

To live at the best that one can be cannot
be achieved if embracing what promotes
the worst inclinations of human-being.

The lower nature doesn't know what to do
with those who live their lives through the
spiritual. It cannot buy them, exploit or
manipulate them; it has no use for them,
to their great advantage.

Where the finite mind sees paradise the
infinite mind sees desert, and vice-versa.

What the higher nature thinks of as something more is what is beyond the temporal

that enhances human life through enlightenment. What the lower nature thinks of is
more of the same banalities that degrade it.

The base ambition demands compromise
after compromise, and in the end, one is left
with nothing. The spiritual demands no
compromise, but then one has everything
that is worth having.

The nourishment of the spiritual is not
lavish in presentation, but more rewarding
and life-nourishing than any table set by
the lower nature.

Who is consciously joined to the eternal
concerns himself with being spiritually

well centered. Who aligns himself with
ambition outside of the spiritual, well
connected to whomever or whatever he
believes will help him in his quest for
earthly advance.

For all its energy, animal nature keeps one
who goes by its rule from coming to life.

There is a self-reliance of ego, and a Self
reliance of the spiritual. One is false, the
other, of truth.

The outside of ego is hard, but its inside is
weak and hollow. The outside of humility
is soft, but its inside is strong and full.

Human Natures

The crux of interior health is a purity of heart, enjoyed solely in the spiritual of human-being.

To allow an untamed animal to roam freely in one's house would be tantamount to allowing the animal to take it over. (The same with the inner house.)

Animals of the wild can be graceful in motion, but no motion of human animality outside the body can be of grace.

The lower nature is primarily interested in self-gratification. The higher, in realization of the spiritual.

of Animal and Spiritual

No more than an antelope cares for a
Mercedes-Benz does the animal of human-
being care for truth and wisdom.

Earthly wealth well serves the world only
when it is administered by wealth of the
higher nature.

The animal of human-being has not its prints
on the greater gifts to humanity.

What is done through the spiritual is given
back to the spiritual.

A spirit is as open as it is humble, as humble as it is open.

As spiritual consciousness grows, all that is good in the life that it has opened follows in growth.

Who says no to selfishness says no to animal sovereignty of his or her life.

The lower nature is skilled at getting what it wants, is well versed in the trade of scheme and manipulation to achieve its aims. But what of them? Centering on interests that are base and shallow with coarse ambition heading their pursuit. And so: could one living by rule of animal-being be considered, in the broader appreciation (or broadest examination) to be an *intelligent* person when the preponderance of his mental prowess beyond securing the needs for survival is recruited to the service of what is by all objective criteria, of a base and shallow character?

What is behind the goals of the lower nature can never rise above the base, and if the motive is base, could the goal, or what is done in the effort to procure it ever be noble?

The lower nature cannot act nobly, cannot give selflessly, cannot be fair, just, trustworthy at all times and in all ways in any relation, because it cannot love (for love is of a depth [a height] of which the lower nature is not endowed).

As certain traits are found on one side of the brain and not the other, so is love to be found only on the spiritual side of human-being.

The spiritual nature goes with an entourage of kindness, forbearance, compassion and generosity, directed by love.

It takes time to recognize the full measure of a person, but not the predominant nature through which the operations of his or her life are set forth.

As parents who are of good spiritual health sincerely desire for their children to go further

than they have gone and do what they can
to aid them in their aspirations, so those
who live through the higher nature are open
to doing what they can for anyone who is
serious about human development, even
those (especially those) with the potential
to go further than they are able to go.

Like a fountain does love flow from where
ego is not.

The sense-awareness of spiritual-being is as
keen as the senses of the gainful predator of
the jungle, but is not used for animal purpose.
It detects weakness, but moves to help, not
to exploit or take advantage of those who
are vulnerable.

Human Natures

Only one who is controlled by animal nature seeks to control others, or some segment(s) of their lives.

Ones who operate through the lower nature assess their strength by how much they're able to dominate and intimidate, and have their way. Through the spiritual, by how much they are able to help, to heal, to constructively serve and create.

Animality rules the temporal. To be a player requires an adherence to its ways.

Not with pomp and circumstance, but with service through reverence and gratitude does the spiritual nature celebrate Life.

of Animal and Spiritual

Advanced is the spirit of those who are
grateful for what they are given; more so
the spirit of those grateful for what they
are able to give.

True compassion is in consistency of living
and performance through the spiritual of
one's life, not an occasional turn and step
toward what is higher, then around and
back into the callosity of the lower levels
of human-being.

The better way is that which produces the
greater treasure ... (the eternal treasure).

Freeing oneself from bondage to the temporal
cannot be a magician's trick — it needs to be
real to connect to what is real.

Human Natures

It is folly to assume that if one works hard
one deserves a good share of life's wealth.
The question is: what is the nature of the
work, and *what is one working for*?

Whatever the degree of education, one who
is subject to animal nature is more trained
than educated, more indoctrinated into a set
of established customs and beliefs than he is
prone to using his eyes to see what *he* sees,
his mind to think what *he* thinks of what is
right and just, and what leads to the more
noble life.

Void of the sentimental, though of deep
feeling and sympathy is the heart guided
by the spiritual.

of Animal and Spiritual

Greater depth means greater sensitivity, means greater consciousness, which means greater awareness, opening the way to greater life — all to be realized through the higher nature.

The life controlled by animal nature is in one form or other the promoting and puffing up of "I."

Not to be exalted in person, but to experience an elevation of life is the goal of the elevated spirit.

When one understands that he breathes for the sake of other, he has aspired to something more than human-animal-being.

A truth that many unfortunately fail to learn
is that joy is withheld, deep happiness is
withheld until one contributes to the joy
and happiness of others.

A child who is lost knows that he is lost, and
feels a need to find or be found. Many adults
lost in the illusions of the temporal, oblivious
to the true calling of human life do not sense
their predicament, living without awareness
that they're in the dark, that the spiritual is
not the guiding force of their lives.

Ego, defender of the false, must be defeated
before a life of truth, in Truth, can begin.

of Animal and Spiritual

How much time is wasted by considerable numbers of youth nearing the age of adulthood who believe themselves to be special, of high importance, simply because they exist, who've yet to begin honing the skills for contributive achievement, or learning the most important lesson of all, that nothing of real value can be made of a human life until ego has been put to rest.

The egoist is like one who is dreaming, seeing himself on top of a mountain ... to wake from the dream is to face the reality of standing at its base.

Who makes his life about himself makes it about nothing, for then it is about ego, and ego is nothing.

Human Natures

All have a light within, but if living through the lower nature it is of no more benefit than a flashlight lying at the bottom of the sea.

Of the myriad of earth's life forms, humans have the unique capacity to face themselves; and one cannot be human in the higher form, cannot turn from animal to human spiritual until this is done.

To grow is to engage one's life — to confront what needs to be corrected, altered or eliminated through diligence of the inner work.

The process of transformation is not without pains, but they are essential to the goal of transcendence.

of Animal and Spiritual

An honest analysis of the destructive procliv-
ities of animal nature can be wounding in its
effect, though such experiences are necessary
to set one's life on to spiritual healing.

The value of the wound spiritually speaking
is, though certain to induce some measure
of pain, it opens awareness, expands
consciousness, the expansion remaining
beyond the healing.

One is given a lifetime to shed the dominant
influence of the lower nature of his life —
and what has he learned that is worth knowing who has not done this? What does he
have that is worth passing on to others that
will be helpful to their awakening to the
better of their lives, except an example of
how not to live, and how tragic it is to
conclude life's journey still enslaved to
the baser impulses of human-being.

Human Natures

In the outer world an enduring peace cannot be achieved through conflict, but in the inner world a lasting peace of strength cannot be realized without it — without going through the battle of animal versus spiritual for the counsellorship of one's life.

If it were possible to have entered into every battle of every war that's been fought since the beginning of human time, yet one avoided the battle that would set one free from animal control of one's life, would be to not have engaged in the only battle for both individual and humankind that counts.

The world suffers more than it has to when man suffers less than he needs to — (i.e. when refusing to accept the kinds of suffering that too many have thus far been unwilling to accept in order to reach the higher nature).

of Animal and Spiritual

There are sufferings that cleanse and purify,
known to the lives that open to their gifts
when they arrive that lead to insight, the
insight, to wisdom, the wisdom, to the
eternal of beauty and love.

No sacrament or ritual of a religion births one
into the spiritual. It is by will and commitment
to do what is required in working toward release
from subjugation to animal command where at
the threshold of spiritualization birth of a new
life begins. (And from that birth, able to be
born again, and again, to higher gradations
of spiritual entity.)

The animality in man is without condition,
not needing to be earned. All stages beyond
it that ultimately lead to the transcendence
of animal nature need to be earned.

Human Natures

In the temporal one exists only to die. In the spiritual one dies to the temporal, to the animal, so one may know of *life*.

What is born brings many things, among them, pain, and from the pain more is brought [great beauty may be brought] into being.

In human character, weeds grow well enough on their own — the flowers must be cultivated if they are to bloom.

As unwanted shrub may be removed from gardens of the earth, so may the unwanted be removed from gardens within.

of Animal and Spiritual

Of even the saints, the spiritual nature is not
predominant at the beginning of their lives,
the animal impulse present here as well,
inclining behavior toward its will — (not
needing to be learned, only given in to).

As the artist shapes his material into a coher-
ence of beauty and meaning, so can a human
being shape his or her life into something
that exemplifies the best of human-being.

A human life is as a cell in the Body of
Humankind. How healthy or toxic that cell
will be is up to the individual.

The spiritual is not only the saving grace,
but the saving cause of humanity.

Human Natures

Where there are excuses the work of spiritual
growth has yet to begin. (Only from the
animal side of man comes the excuse.)

Even the advanced spirit is raw material
for the creation of something better ... of
something more.

Once the choice has been made to go the
way of the spiritual there is no choice as to
what must be done to aspire to higher stages
of growth.

The spiritual is most demanding, but also
most rewarding.

of Animal and Spiritual

Spirituality is not about making one's life
easier, but stronger, deeper, richer, more
vital and intense, to be made in ways harder,
though always doing what one can to lessen
the burdens of others.

There is no such happening as a "death bed
conversion" from animal nature to spiritual.
Though one could have a feeling of what
the essence of spirituality is in one's final
moments, it could not convey what it is to
spend a life ever growing through inner work,
becoming more kind, more humble and
compassionate as the years pass, learning
what it means to live a truly spiritual life.

One shows gratitude or ingratitude for the
life one is given by how it is lived.

Human Natures

To know by what nature a person is being guided, no further need one look than the state of his or her heart.

The stronger the noble of spirit grow, the more humble they become. The more the ego-driven weaken, the more coarse and imperious becomes their way of manner.

A gladness of heart can only be where there is a genuine goodness of heart.

With each act of goodness something is added to one's spiritual wealth.

of Animal and Spiritual

People who live through the spiritual are not
interested in how many will know of them
by their deeds, but in how many will benefit
by them.

The higher wealth is realized through the higher
nature, by those who wish to share it, to give
all they can of it, living as a vessel of light.

Those from all ages who lived their lives in
the eternal (in the spiritual) would, if brought
together, be able to easily converse, would
feel a kinship, as if they had always known
one another, be it one from the second
century greeting another from the twenty-
first. Those who staked their lives in the
temporal given to animal rule would feel
more like strangers, having only the events
of their time to share, the separation of
centuries preventing them from relating to
their brethren with the instant recognition

and quality of association of the former
assembly, living through and for, what is
true and always.

Cultural barriers are impossible to break
when living through the temporal. It is those
who live through the eternal who can open
to all cultures with a pure heart, free of ego
fears and aggressions.

Above the discords of animal-natured life
sound the harmonies of spiritual love.

The lower nature takes ignorance for
knowledge, folly for wisdom, and darkness
for light — like taking the moon for the sun.

of Animal and Spiritual

One is lost until the spiritual of one's life
has won.

So much of the human world is not only
alien to its highest aspirations, but also mur-
derous, stunted by the rule of animal-being.

Because of the predominance of animal
influence over humankind, it has always
undervalued the highest things — which
are in truth beyond value ... (and to under
value is to undermine).

Self-esteem, self-confidence, self-"love":
much praised and espoused by multitudes
while of self-criticism little in comparison is

spoken, and rarer still the example of, often missing where warranted despite the importance of its presence throughout for the sake of humanity.

Like a glimpse of sunlight gleaming through a hole of a darkened prison cell, one who stirs with discontent from the baseness that permeates much of human endeavor discerns the possibility of what human life can be beyond futility, achieved with courage, fortitude, discipline, temperance, and love.

Many who align themselves with animal-being speak of a reverence for life when they can experience no more than a living death, for that is all the lower nature is or can be about — confined to a self-centeredness, immersed in the temporal, filled with illusion and dissolution, with every gain turning to dust.

of Animal and Spiritual

The needs of the noble spirit can be simply
stated as the need to love, the need to give,
the need to grow. The selfish wants of the
lower nature are of a list too numerous
to state.

Ego holds claim to the life that operates
through temporal-being; only the humble
can know a presence of eternal-being.

The ultimate courage is a willingness to be
broken by forces of the eternal that beckon
one to grow, whose mission is the termination
of ego.

The price of the power of Self is the giving
over of one's life to selflessness.

Human Natures

To live without ego is to live without shield,
but with the strongest of armor.

In the absence of ego you are free to join
with the eternal without barrier of "I," of
"me," now in union with eternity.

The selfless spirit is humble in its power
and powerful in its humility.

To "have a life" is not the primary interest
of those who serve Life, for to so serve is to
be of Life — to be consciously connected
to the everlasting, which is so much more
than having a life of the fleeting.

Love and truth are present in the temporal,
but are not of the temporal.

It is the connection to the world free of selfish
inclination that makes for contribution of the
greater expanse.

From the lower nature comes the preoccupa-
tion with trying to convince others that one
is Somebody. To live through the spiritual
is to have one's focus on how one may be
of assistance, ready to serve wherever one
happens to be.

Those who dedicate themselves to the realization of human potential are not obsessed with
the question of how successful they are from

a worldly view, but how effective and productive they are. Not consumed with how much they're at peace with themselves, but what they are doing to help bring about a more peaceful world.

The make-up of spiritual nature enables if necessary the strength to stand alone for what most needs to be stood for.

It is not possible for anyone living truly through the spiritual to *fear* another ruled by animal nature, only to be concerned for what he could do to jeopardize the work in service or progress that is of the spiritual.

The ways of the worldly are of scheme and compromise, pure and simple — (but their operations are far from pure, and the problems they create, far from simple).

No matter what direction a majority takes there is always choice for an individual as to how one is to live regarding one's principles.

Like something priceless hidden inside a home unbeknownst to its occupant, what is most precious in an individual can be lost when not engaged in work championing the spiritual dimension of human life.

Before becoming rich in spirituality one must become poor in human animality that strays outside the physical.

Human Natures

Like all organisms of the earth the human
being has needs that must be met to sustain a
viable life, but unlike other life forms in their
natural setting, these needs can be indulged
to excess, which move outside of need into
greedful want — often at the expense of
whatever else, the appetency for more than is
needed extending into territory available to no
other species, yet still carrying the identity of
animality, played out in a host of ambitions
that lead to naught.

True progress is not possible in a life ruled by
the lower nature, for like the howl of many a
beast, it makes fierce noise at ground level
but is without wings and not able to rise.

The valid contribution to the world is what
is incorruptible, achieved only through the
spiritual.

The interest of the lower nature is not in constructive inner work, but in devious outer play.

Depth is not necessary for baseness to set up shop and put forth its operations. To the bringing forth of nobility it is principal.

Virtue over self-interest is the mark of the noble spirit.

A strong structure doesn't cave in or crumble when elements of Nature pass its way, and so the strong spiritual character when pressure mounts to do what is foreign to its nature.

Human Natures

Good to others are those of noble character, though one of such character doesn't forgo principle to be in the good graces of another.

It is only when administering through the spiritual that life can be honored in human form.

A human life executing through the lower nature displays sickness of soul, a darkness of mind, and a poverty of heart.

When encountering arrogance, one is in the presence of animal nature; when encountering greed and selfishness, one is in the presence of animal nature; when encountering malice and cruelty, one is in the presence of animal nature.

of Animal and Spiritual

The use and abuse of others is a most
evil expenditure of life's time, commonly
practiced by the animal side of man.

There is a difference between being of *use*
to others, and being of service to them.
(The lower nature on the receiving end of
the former; the spiritual, the giving end
of the latter.)

The motto of animal-being spoken in gesture
and deed is: "What I want before the better
need of all else."

Though an action may inadvertently produce
a positive in the result, a deed of goodness
must always be one of selflessness.

Human Natures

In the scope of ego presence acquaintance-ship abounds, but not friendship.

There is more self-serving in the world than there is service of a selfless nature.

More examples are there of what to avoid in human conduct than what to embrace.

The selfless life is an oasis in the many desert lands of humanity.

Besides the worst of underhandedness there is flattery, fawning, offers of favor around worldly ambition, but no true generosity.

Much of what enables the climbing of worldly ladders prevents the scaling of spiritual heights.

The lower nature often moves to procure what it is ill equipped to utilize well — (eg. positions of authority and influence).

Independence from material need may be achieved in the absence of noble procedure,

but nobility of spirit cannot be without
distance from what is compromising to
the spiritual.

Those guided by the better nature can
gladly give of their lives a world of sacrifice
for the higher good; ones dwelling at the
lower base of animal-being would think
nothing of sacrificing the world for a yield
of short-lived gain.

Who lives through the spiritual cannot help
but live today in a manner that tomorrow
it will not be something to give pause to or
be ashamed of, but be an example to continue
to follow.

of Animal and Spiritual

Animal human can live without compassion, magnanimity, or yearnings for higher growth; spiritual human cannot be a moment without them.

Those of a pure humanity are interested in helping to liberate people in spiritual poverty from what keeps them from the true treasure of their lives. They are without interest in communications of an intent to beguile or manipulate, or compel others to do anything, especially counter to doing them good.

The higher spirit hopes for others to take the hint; the lower, to take the bait.

Human Natures

Even in the savageries of Nature, life's majesty is not debased. The same cannot be said of the cruelties of the human world generated by the animal of human-being.

Of Nature's brutal dimension there is essentiality in that it is part of what is necessary to maintain its balance. No such benefit is there in the malicious behaviors of man.

Animal nature is not exhibited only by the human brute that resorts to physical means at every turn to have his way, but those as well who do so in more refined ways, many in suit and tie, with advanced degrees and titles to their names.

of Animal and Spiritual

Evil can only exist where there is evil
intent, and no species save for humankind
is capable of this.

Through inexperience and naiveté errors
are made, and though the neophyte be
responsible for the honest mistake, it is
excusable. But the knowing and willful
malice, though such may be forgiven,
can never be excused.

A person need not do more than present
an excellence of some kind to be despised,
such is the response from the virulence of
envy, among the more vile traits of human-
animal-being.

Human Natures

Their inner gardens cannot be beautiful who'd wish to trample on the spiritual gardens of others.

To not be able to feel joy in one's life is tragic, but more so is the inability to rejoice in the well earned joy of another.

When in surroundings where there's a void of amenities the higher spirit is prone to be more giving for all to help compensate for the dearth of humaneness.

If wronged by another, those who reflect through spiritual consciousness include in

their time of reflection on the incident
whether they've ever treated anyone in a
similar fashion, and if so, vow to their best
to never again behave toward others in
such a manner.

One person is viciously abused, yet treats
others with benevolence; another is treated
with the utmost courtesy, yet deals to others
meanness and contempt — so may be the
difference between the conduct of spiritual
human and animal human.

To oblige or encourage someone in a
pernicious attack or maneuver against
another is to partake in its evil, taking
share in responsibility for the immoral
crime.

Human Natures

To not take pleasure in even the slightest
embarrassment or humiliation of anyone is a
sign that one's character has raised its head
from the shadowed ground of animal nature
to the light of the spiritual.

Like greed, cruelty closes off, feeding on
its wretchedness, but what damage it does
to the world.

All that is good cannot seed and manifest
without the aid of courage, but most evils
are of weakness moved by cowardice.

An honored resolve to not add evils to the world is in itself a substantial good.

It is easier to handle a cub of the wild than the animal it will become — so too the base elements of the animal of man.

How different the consequences for life are inside and out, of liberties exercised by the lower nature from those by the spiritual.

They remain as children in the poorest sense who do not engage the pains of higher growth.

Human Natures

Sufferings harden, yet weaken the spirit
of those ruled by the lower nature; soften,
yet strengthen those whose core is not of
the animal.

When the higher spirit is pained it seeks
not to revenge on life, but works to give it
in return the best it is able, produced and
delivered with love.

It makes all the difference when one has an
inner sanctum to transform sufferings into
positives, made possible through strength
of the spiritual nature.

of Animal and Spiritual

Only the spiritual can be selfless and compassionate, and only from such living can benefit be given to all.

Magnanimity is a property of the rich of heart, compliments of the higher nature.

The lower nature can best be defined not by what it has but what it hasn't, which is a true and constant reverence for other.

The world can be at times torturous to the sensitive spirit, strongly aware of the many knaveries and iniquities active throughout it,

yet still goes through life's journey with
sympathy and love, doing what can be done
to abate them and ease the strife of those
whom they afflict.

Love doesn't turn a blind eye to the evils
that debase humankind; it faces them, and
the extent of their mayhem, and the cost
of denying them.

Every time an injustice is ignored or a moral
imperative fails to be acted on, a part of
humanity's soul is scarred.

Those who process and assimilate through
spiritual consciousness are not interested in

who is right, but what is right — they do not
play favorites or accommodate bias in an
examination of truth. Those closest to them
have no advantage over those most distant
in their determination of what is false, and
what is true.

Even when outraged by the inanities of the
world the denouncements from the spiritual
are put forth with love.

Maturity of the higher order is not achieved
until one's concern for the whole of humankind is as vital as the concern for one's
person, or one's person and family, or one's
family and community, for less than this is
to not be thinking wisely or humanely.

Human Natures

Who never acts unless there is something
in it for himself always goes away with
nothing, no matter what is received.

The search for happiness is itself one of
selfish impulse, and therefore manifest of the
lower nature. Who concentrates on helping
others need not search, for it flowers from
within when the life one has been given is
lived to give in return.

In the best moments of one living through
the higher nature, when the whole of one's
strength is focused on worthy endeavor
that benefits the world, when purpose is
being revealed, one is reminded of what
happiness is.

of Animal and Spiritual

All may not know a genius of the mind,
may not have a phenomenal mental gift or
produce exceptional achievement in science
or the arts, but all may know (may earn) a
genius of the heart through a persistence of
inner work accompanied by humility.

Nobility and humbleness go hand-in-hand . . .
(one might say are the working hands of
the spiritual).

To live to contribute in union with ideals
that transcend the temporal is to connect
to a power that allows for transition into
progressive stages of spiritual realization.

Human Natures

All are born with the ability to give
darkness to the world. Not everyone
ends life's journey with having worked
to the power that frees the inner light.

Selfishness, the pride of ego, can be nothing
but enemy to the best of human life.

To be aware of others; to be considerate of
others; to be of benefit to others ... this,
the way of the higher spirit.

Love isn't something that is turned on and
off. It is at all times abiding and open in a

life, or is not. (And where the smallest trace
of ego is present, love will not be found.)

In true humility there is nothing to prove,
nothing to want having to do with manipulation or control of others, no solicitations
that work to one's favor in pursuit of the
base, for here the impetus that moves one
to such endeavor does not exist.

For those who live by the spiritual, fairness
is always an issue as to how they deal with
others, though not for those who have
dealings with them regarding the fairness
they are sure to be given.

Human Natures

To behave consistently in a just and honest
fashion; to not take advantage when it would
be most easy to do in the many ways that
avail themselves in opportunity, is to behave
in a manner contrary to the collective leaning
of human character in its current stage of
evolution. This, a triumph of the spiritual
over the animal of human-being.

Man deserves to be free so far as he takes
responsibility for his freedom and doesn't
misuse it by abusing others with selfish
exploits of the lower nature.

It is no small show of baseness to take
advantage in any measure of another's
innocence.

of Animal and Spiritual

The noble of spirit honor the trust that others give to them, and add to it a grace of compassion.

A reliable goodness cannot fail to be present in the life whose primary interest is to serve the eternal good.

The animal dominance of a human life tightens with age, steadily hardening into the trivial and base. The spiritual grows in awareness and love, deepening in sensitivity to what needs to be given, and what it is able to give.

Human Natures

Whatever its fate, the animal of the wild
dies with more dignity than the human
whose allegiance through all his days
was to the animal of his being.

The lower nature bears no shame for its
baseness; the higher, no hubris for the
power of its love.

The light is always on in the spiritual life
to be of service to those in need of help
who are open to what it has to give, be
they friend, stranger or foe.

of Animal and Spiritual

It is when one has aspired to a stage of development where he wouldn't wish the least of his afflictions on a worst enemy that he has reached the heart of true empathy.

The more spiritually evolved are saddened by the pains that afflict others more than by their own; they rejoice in the good fortunes of others, as if they were their own.

They do not deserve compassion who are indifferent to the sufferings of others. Still, the spiritual nature gives it to them, because it is incapable of not giving it.

Human Natures

The noble of spirit need not bond with others to help them, to do for them, to give generously of their lives to them.

The highest compassion is that which is given to all without the need of motivation behind the giving that everything is One, which one is a part of — (this need, not free of self-interest).

Not to cling to a particular in a narrow, personalized way, but to gaze at the whole with deep empathy ... this is the egoless state.

Without ego the whole may be embraced.

of Animal and Spiritual

It is only in spiritual detachment that a
compassion of the highest order can be,
for then it is of a universal quality beyond
the personal or sentimental, with the measure
and objectivity necessary to be of service to
all, where and when it is needed.

The smaller the creature within the sphere
of one's compassion the greater one's heart,
the greater the compassion.

Of the state of a human life the heart has
the final say, spoken by the higher or lower
nature, according to how it has lived.

Human Natures

The shadow of the lower nature is large,
though the measure of its character is small.

The lower nature does for only its interests;
the higher, for the better interest of all.

Who lives for his own interests, believing
that life is about doing and getting all he can
for himself, or himself and close relations,
indifferent to the plight of the world and the
magnitude of work that needs to be done, for
which all humans, to the full scale of their
ability are responsible, is like someone who
enters a town that has just experienced a
catastrophe with people everywhere in need
of help, who gives no regard to this, looking
instead for a nice place to dine and drink, and
wondering about entertainments the town has
to offer.

of Animal and Spiritual

For a human life there needs to be more than living through animal-being, otherwise something is missed beyond the extraordinary.

Subjectively speaking, it is a choice if one is to live through the spiritual in service to life; objectively, is it not a duty?

When a child's eyes fully open they do so with wonder. The journey through life has been purposeful if the closing of the eyes is with the serenity of spirit known to those who have served life well.

Joined through the spiritual as one are empathy and love.

Without the will to love, the will to live is but the will of animality.

Life, feeding on life . . . in play in the human world as in the wilds of Nature — but the feeding in the human world is more than of the body . . . it is the feeding on [the diminishing of] the human soul.

In view of the inevitable passing of what allows for a life experience of the profound, should it not be always for a human being a matter of making the most of it, this achieved by turning one's attention to the best that is offered, which is and of the eternal.

More important than to "rage against the dying of the light"[1] as the end is drawing near is to decry the darkening of the light that goes on daily in the presence of life, that has been going on throughout the history of humankind (and never more than in modern times), the impetus of animality wielding the leading influence over human behavior, preventing the highest aspirations from being attained, the full power of the spiritual holding the promise of humanity, unable to do what it can do, be what it can be to the world because a majority have settled for so much less than what could be experienced.

1 Thomas, Dylan 1952, "Do Not Go Gentle into that Good Night."

Human Natures

The spiritual is what is ever young, the
true fountain of youth, ready to accord
blessing after blessing, to replace the
hollow mendacity of the lower nature
with a veritable life of enduring strength
and love, transcendent of the ephemeral,
free of the futile and vain, offering not
only a better way, but the only way to
the realization of what it is to be more
than a vassal of animal entity.

In the midst of worldly insanities, one must
find one's way to sanity; in the midst of
worldly follies, one must find one's way to
wisdom; in the midst of worldly falsehoods,
one must find one's way to truth; in the
midst of worldly hatreds, one must find
one's way to love — through guidance
of the higher nature.

of Animal and Spiritual

What would human life be without the spiritual dimension? What the universe would be without the stars.

The miracle of humankind is in the remarkable gift it is blessed with that no other life on earth is given — the opportunity to rise from animal to spiritual, even to the heights of sainthood, the human spirit calling humanity to something more, to attain the standard of being that it is able, to recognize that what a species can be is what it is meant to be, that the greatest enlightenment offered to the human world cannot be realized without the will to reverse the prevailing order of the best of human conduct from what is now the exception to becoming the rule, that what individuals have achieved through the ages in spiritual progression, humankind must find its way to do if it is to claim its rightful destiny.

Epilogue

There was a time when our distant ancestors were in constant danger of being killed by ferocious animals and other deadly predators, forcing upon them a critical need to be ever vigilant of their surroundings for whatever they might encounter that would be perilous to their lives. Imagine the degree of sense-awareness, the keenness of instincts and skills that had to be developed just to stay alive. The successful acquirement of these necessities not only saved them from extinction, but enabled them to evolve to where they would eventually become the sovereign life on earth.

But this was primarily animal outthinking animal — in such a brutal climate, the animal ways of negotiating the hazardous terrain of life or death required a facility superior to that of other animals to rise to the top rank of their environment.

The problem that man is presently faced with is that the very cunning and self-interest based impetus that was so necessary at one time for the survival of the human species is what can now destroy it.

Humankind can no longer afford the postponement of taking the next step in its evolution, to move away from animality and into the spiritual of human-being (i.e. a spirituality that is truly lived and is not the property of any theology or religious sect or denomination). This will be as challenging, perhaps in ways even more so, as the demands that had to be met by our forbearers — the rule of venture going from exploiting the outer world with disregard to turning inward to what lies deeper than ego, to the enlightenment of selflessness, and all that this would do toward the realization of a humanity that has only been dreamed of.

A major hindrance to such an advance is the danger having been virtually removed of humans being annihilated at any hour by the predacity of Nature — fear of attack by creatures armed with fang and claw of the kind experienced by contemporaries of a primitive age and what was at stake now foreign and without meaning to the present age. And though inarguably an important and welcomed feat of eradication that made way for the transpiring of many benefits in human history, the point to be stated as to its influence on human development is there are negatives that have generated from the result that are counterproductive to the current need for spiritual

growth, mainly, the remaining presence
of the selfish impulse minus the powerful
drive to evolve or perish that was once the
central priority in the collective psyche of
the species.

In fact, with all the assumed comforts
of modern life encouraged and aggressively
promoted by the affluent nations, many have
been lulled into an enervation of sloth and
weakness, opening themselves only to what
promises to make life "easier," to whatever
will spare them the burden of building true
character, of doing the hard work that needs
to be done to take their lives to the next level,
going instead in the opposite direction —
one that allows a malignancy of numerous
perversions to exist that bear among them the
deliberate burning of rain forests and other
environmental horrors, and daily deaths of
children by the thousands from disease and
starvation that could not be tolerated if this
shame were widely recognized and addressed
through spiritual consciousness.

What do developments in technologies,
science, economics, or anything else matter
until such evils are unacceptable and cease
to be allowed to continue?

Dangers have been eliminated from the
human world, but new ones have emerged
to take their place. Threats to the survival

of ancient ancestors came from without; the dangers to human survival today are from within — the greed, the depravity, the self-indulgence, the veneration of mediocrity so damaging to humanity and of increasing detriment to the globe it inhabits.

What labors are endeavored to solve the problems that afflict humankind consistently go to stemming their outgrowth or treatment of symptoms instead of the cause, which is why no change for the better is ever safe from being eroded and seldom holds for long (and never with the strength or inspired advocacy that was present at its inception).

Officials of governments enter and leave office, elected and unelected, taking or given authority for a time of managing a nation's affairs, and of even the best of systems founded on the basis of shared powers of governance in support of noble ideals, their intention is duly honored only in rare moments when politics and narrow interests are put aside for the interest of the citizenry, creating the illusion of a turning point, a substantial difference made where rhetoric and obstacle have been overcome to clear the way for progress to proceed toward a future free of the demoralizations of the past and favorable to what is right and just for all, then after a while the same unrests surface as before, though sometimes with a different face, and there is confoundment, and wonder of the reason, charge and countercharge, and calls for explanation.

It is because the principal change that needs to occur is the shifting of attention to where the investment of effort to bring about a true transformation must be applied, to doing the work that holds the solution to creating a foundation for a prosperity of an enlightened nature that can be built upon, which is the inner work, starting with engaging the corruptions that sabotage all attempts to deal with human problems when the focus is not on the root of the trouble.

From the dawn of recorded history the members of the human play have changed, the props (technologies) have changed, but the play remains unchanged, analogous to a chaotic dream void of order and progression, in motion, but not moving forward, the human world ever plagued by the same moral failings in consequence of it being easier to convince ourselves that the source of obstruction is external than to face the truth that it is rooted inside and therein must be addressed, individual by individual, in numbers far greater than have taken up the challenge in any age or generation if there is to be improvement in human behavior of the scale necessary for humankind to move onward as a species into a living spirituality.

When the human race was of a measure that was considerably less in numerical degree, and had well attained the proficiency to cope with the most menacing of outer dangers and still safe from the ability to destroy itself, its survival was not a concern. But now, with the count of its population in the billions and rising, and means at its disposal able to cause destruction beyond imagining with its lower nature as broadly in command as ever of its operations that today include policy of global impact, it is crucial that the next phase of human evolution be commenced in a serious way, if the chance is not to be lost for doing what is needed in time to ensure a future of promise for humankind.

Index

Index

Index

Index

Index

Index

Index

Index

There is always hope for the individual to aspire to what human life can be — to experience its heights, its depths, its ecstasies.

Notes

ABOUT THE AUTHOR

Carroll Blair is the author of more than twenty books, including five volumes of poetry. His work has been favorably reviewed, as illustrated by the following commentary from Midwest Book Review, which proclaimed, *"The poetic expression of Carroll Blair is both unique and compelling. Using word images like the strokes of a painter's brush, Blair creates a resonating recognition that is the mark of a master poet."* An alumnus of the Boston Conservatory, he graduated summa cum laude with a degree in music composition. He now lives in northern Massachusetts working on material for future publications and cultivating a philosophy of human evolution through inner growth, the essence of that philosophy presented in *Human Natures, of Animal and Spiritual*.